CW01095837

Assessment for learning

learning

Digital tools for effective practice

Sally Betts and Alastair Clark

niace

promoting adult learning

ⓝiace
promoting adult learning

©2008 National Institute of Adult Continuing Education
(England and Wales)
21 De Montfort Street
Leicester
LE1 7GE

Company registration no. 2603322
Charity registration no. 1002775

Cataloguing in Publication Data
A CIP record of this title is available from the British Library
Designed and typeset by Book Production Services, London
Printed and bound in the UK by Latimer Trend

ISBN: 978 1 86201 370 4

Contents

Acknowledgements

The authors would like to thank the following people for their contribution to this publication:

Alistair McNaught
Di Dawson
Judith Gawn
Maria Kambouri
Peter Lavender
Nigel Ecclesfield
Steve Glennon
Terry Loane

We would also like to give thanks to those who showed us how assessment for learning works in practice: Kathy Cockcroft, Julie Cull, Nina Cullaine, Sheila Dodds, Jo Duckett, Judy Evans, Tracy Hewitt, Elaine Husselby, Sally Jowers and Susannah Redman.

We are grateful for permission to reproduce images supplied by Techdis and the Museums, Libraries and Archives Council.

Finally, the authors would like to thank some of their own colleagues who have helped to make the publication possible: Gemma Hammond, Shubhanna Hussain-Ahmed, Peter Lavender and Tracy Slawson.

1

Introduction

Teachers are increasingly interested in developing their understanding of how they can use regular assessment with their learners to inform and improve learning programmes. This 'assessment for learning' takes place throughout a course of study, and this e-guideline sets out to explore how digital tools and e-learning methods can be useful in the process.

Assessment can have several functions: it can be used in education as a way of measuring attainment of learners in order to provide evidence for qualifications or to provide a way of comparing institutions. This 'assessment of learning' is very important but very different to what is covered here. This book focuses only on 'assessment for learning', which is carried out by teachers with their learners as part of the learning process.

The work of Black and Wiliam and others (Black et al., 2003) has given 'assessment for learning' a high profile; their work will be considered in the next chapter. In addition, many practitioners in adult learning are familiar with applying the five-staged process for 'Recognising and Recording Progress and Achievement' (RARPA). This system was endorsed by the Learning and Skills Council (LSC) originally for non-accredited learning. The RARPA process recognises three types of assessment: Initial (RARPA stage 2), Formative (RARPA stage 4), and finally Summative (RARPA stage 5).

It is ongoing 'formative' assessment during a course that constitutes assessment for learning. As the RARPA process acknowledges, this has two elements: the checking of progress and feedback to learners. This book will concern itself with ways of checking progress and methods of providing feedback to develop and enrich the dialogue between learner and teacher in order to improve the learning.

Five stages of the RARPA process

(Recognising and Recording Progress and Achievement)

1. Course aims that are clearly stated.
2. Initial assessment of learners' starting points and needs.
3. Discussion and negotiation to identify appropriately challenging objectives.
4. Formative assessment, checking on progress and giving feedback.
5. Final recognition of progress, recording and celebration of achievement – summative assessment.

Source: 'Recognising and recording progress and achievement in non-accredited learning'. M. Greenwood, P Wilson. LSC, NIACE 2004

There is considerable interest in the use of e-learning methods for assessment and the NIACE publication Signalling Success (Clark and Hussain-Ahmed, 2006) looked at their use for the RARPA process. In training sessions run by NIACE on this topic the greatest interest amongst practitioners was for stage 4 of RARPA – the formative assessment stage. This is longest stage and has most to contribute to improving the quality of the teaching and learning.

Digital learning methods can add a great deal of flexibility to this process. For example, by using portable devices such as a digital video camera or voice recorder, assessment can occur wherever it is needed, not just in the classroom. A learner can record, at home, their performance of a skill such as cooking a dish learnt in class, reading a story to a child, or even using a software application. Just as assessment itself must fit seamlessly into the learning process, so choice of technology and the way that it is presented are both crucial to ensuring that the technology provides a positive enhancement to the learning and does not create barriers or resistance. Through careful choice of an appropriate digital method it is possible to get an insight into the learner's thought processes whilst performing a learning activity.

Two other terms are used to differentiate types of assessment: 'high stakes' and 'low stakes' assessment. 'High stakes' assessments are summative, external assessments whilst 'low stakes' assessments are to encourage student and teacher reflection and are used to inform the teaching and learning process within classrooms. Thus, low stakes assessments are in effect 'assessment for learning'. We have chosen not to use these terms in this book, but readers should be aware that they do appear in literature elsewhere.

In this book will also explore how to use e-portfolios to collect and comment on evidence of achievement. We will look at some accessible methods for producing simple but effective e-portfolios. We will also investigate the practical and ethical issues raised as learners collect increasing amounts of data in diverse forms during their learning journey.

So, this book will focus only on assessment for learning. However, readers should recognise that this may also be referred to as 'formative' or 'low stakes' assessment.

We will draw on evidence from research and examples from practice to provide readers with tools that will help them apply e-learning to enhance the way that they use assessment to engage learners more actively in the learning process.

2

Assessment for learning

This chapter explores how assessment for learning can be developed in the classroom and examines some of the ways that digital methods can be used to help the process. It sets the scene for the later chapters where we will look at these methods in greater detail. We will draw on some important recent research and combine this with examples of practice.

Robert Stakes from the University of Illinois is widely credited with having made this helpful distinction between types of assessment:

When a cook tastes soup, that's formative; when the guests taste the soup, that's summative.

This chapter deals with the 'soup tasting' phase of learning where progress is checked and decisions made about changes that will improve the final result.

Assessment for learning should be informative, engaging and motivating for both learner and tutor alike and allow learners to develop a fuller understanding and enjoyment of their subject.

Recommendations from research studies

The research work of Black and Wiliam looked at how formative assessment could raise attainment in secondary schools. From this research, the Assessment Reform Group was able to produce a list of ten principles shown below.

Good assessment for learning:

1. is part of effective planning;
2. focuses on how students learn;
3. is central to classroom practice;
4. is a key professional skill;
5. has an emotional impact;
6. affects learner motivation;
7. promotes commitment to learning goals and assessment criteria;
8. helps learners know how to improve;
9. encourages self-assessment;
10. recognises all achievements.

(Assessment Reform Group (ARG), 2002)

More recently, the Improving Formative Assessment (IFA) project (2004–2007) explored assessment for learning and identified significant advantages to the learners when assessment is applied so that it transforms the way in which teaching is delivered. The advantages include that learners:

> are fully involved in the whole process of assessment;
> understand why they are being assessed;
> understand the importance of assessment as a tool by which they will identify their weaknesses and improve their skills and ultimately their grades;
> evaluate their own work through self reflection and become reflective learners;
> evaluate the work of others and provide constructive feedback;
> provide positive peer support;
> take control of their own learning, become more autonomous;
> become more motivated and their confidence grows.

'Assessment for learning is important because it aims to encourage learners to take more responsibility for their own learning, to become engaged with the process of assessment in more active ways, and to understand not only what they're learning but how they're learning. It's also important for the purposes of the teacher who can use the results of assessment in order to plan their teaching and to adapt teaching based on the outcomes.

Assessment for learning should lead to a far more personalised learning experience because the assessment is based on a dialogue with learners about learners' needs, about their progress, about gaps in their knowledge and their understanding and their skills. The teachers should use the outcomes of that dialogue in order to plan teaching that addresses the needs of those individual learners and differentiate activities in the classroom in a more individual way.'

Judith Gawn, NIACE – Improving Formative Assessment Project

Engaging in assessment should be seen as an integral part of teachers' practices as it maximises the potential for raising learner achievement and motivation.

The IFA project highlighted six key interventions by teachers, which can make the assessment process work well. These are:

1 engaging learners in constructive dialogue focusing on skills, knowledge, real-life contexts and success criteria

2 inviting learners to draw up their own assessment criteria and devise their own marking schemes

3 providing opportunities for learners to reflect on their own learning

4 providing opportunities for peer assessment

5 applying effective questioning techniques and giving detailed feedback that is more than just a grade/score/mark

6 creating a positive learning environment where learners feel relaxed

(IFA Project 2004-2007)

The challenge for teachers is to decide how best to apply these within their practice and this should include making well informed choices about use of learning technologies.

Technology to support teachers' interventions

Here we will look in more detail at the six areas of intervention suggested by the IFA project and offer initial thoughts on use of technology.

Constructive dialogue focusing on skills, knowledge, real-life contexts and success criteria

In order to plan a programme of study that will engage a learner and enable them to achieve their aims, there has to be an ongoing dialogue between tutor and learner. From the start, the tutor must understand why a learner wants to study and how they intend to apply the skills and knowledge learned. This information can then be used, together with the results of an initial test or quiz; to open up a meaningful conversation about the steps required to achieve the learner's aims. The discussion ought to show a learner the scale of the task involved and should result in the setting of realistic, achievable initial goals. One way in which digital technology can be applied here is to use a handheld audio recorder to capture the conversation without the need to stop and make notes.

The understanding generated in such discussions will help the tutor to deliver learning in a context that is relevant and motivating to the learner.

TIP

You could learn more about your learners' interests, hobbies or work by providing an 'introducing me' template for them to use when completing their profiles on a learning platform.

This deeper insight into the learners will provide contexts that they have prior knowledge of, and find meaningful and interesting.

The dialogue between tutor and learner is ongoing throughout the study. As the learner is assessed, the tutor needs to feed back, focusing on skills and knowledge and guiding the learner to see how they can improve further. Making a summary of this dialogue can help the learner see the path travelled and the achievements made. This summary could be notes in an online learning log or e-portfolio, or perhaps a short voice recording.

Allowing learners to draw up their own assessment criteria and devise their own marking schemes

Learners need to see themselves moving towards their overall goal in order to remain motivated and focused. Tutors continually assess their learners in order to inform future sessions and to provide constructive feedback. However, this process can be far more effective if the learner is engaged in the whole assessment process. By drawing up their own assessment criteria and devising their own marking schemes, learners will be better prepared to understand what they need to do to achieve their goals.

One way to do this is to have a group discussion about a specific task and use mind-mapping software to capture the learners' thoughts on what could be measured, in order to determine if they had successfully achieved the task – the assessment criteria. The tutor can facilitate the discussion using open questions to draw on learners' existing knowledge and experience to draw out important factors that can be measured.

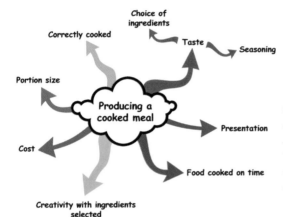

Learners can use mind mapping software to devise their own assessment criteria.

This helps to place the learners at the centre of the assessment process; they take ownership of it and are able to measure themselves and each other against their negotiated assessment criteria. It provides opportunities for peer feedback, as learners fully understand the criteria they are being assessed against.

TIP

A full list of open source and commercial Mind Mapping software can be found on Wikipedia.

A tutor can model giving feedback to a learner and make a video record of it for learners to watch and discuss. The video would demonstrate what is meant by constructive feedback and illustrate the relative importance of comments that focus on the work and those that refer to the person. Watching the video might make the learner aware of the impact that feedback can have on a person, both positive and negative. The learner can watch the video as many times as they like in order to acquire the skills of giving constructive feedback to their peers.

'Tasting and testing'

A tutor found that learners were initially surprised and a little worried by the idea of other people in the class tasting the meals they had just learned to make, but through discussion about the assessment criteria they came to understand why it was important to have peer feedback.

Having watched cookery game-shows on TV and so seen judges' feedback to contestants the learners were able to think of criteria they could be measured against. The tutor found the whole process helped the group to bond, and their support of each other was fostered from the first session. The learners engaged fully in the assessment process and were able to recognise their own successes and areas of weakness.

Providing opportunities for learners to reflect on their own learning

A period of reflection on the learning that has taken place is important in the learning process. It gives learners the opportunity to think about what they have learnt and to consider whether there are still areas that they need to develop further.

Learners need time to consider the impact new skills and knowledge will have on their life, whether at work or home. It might be that learning more about a subject will provide not only skills and knowledge but also change views and attitudes in important ways. Reflection will help learners to recognise this kind of change.

It is also important for a learner to reflect on the way in which they are learning and to decide which methods worked best for them. Understanding this helps to develop the skills needed to become an independent learner.

In a classroom situation, learners are often asked to reflect at the end of a session on the learning that has taken place during the class. However, each learner will approach this differently and some will need more reflection time than others. Technology provides learners with ways of stimulating reflection and provides flexible opportunities to capture reflective thoughts. For example, many of our learners now have a mobile phone with a camera and a voice recorder. These can be used to collect images of learning activities to stimulate reflective thoughts which can then spoken into the voice recorder.

Online journals and blogs enable learners to reflect outside of the classroom and at a time more appropriate to them. They can keep their reflections private or share them with their tutor and peers, allowing their thoughts to open up further discussions. For some learners, being able to discuss their learning with others helps them to reflect and the use of online forums can facilitate this process.

As all the learners on the NVQ plumbing course had mobile phones, the tutor asked them to use the 'Record' function to collect their reflective thoughts during the week. He encouraged them to reflect on the skills they applied during the week, both the successful applications and those those that showed further work was needed. He also asked them to record any new skills they thought they needed. Their recordings were reviewed and discussed during the session. Learners could text any recording to the tutor if they wanted to make him aware of something before the next session.

Providing opportunities for peer assessment

In any classroom situation constructive feedback from the tutor is essential, but feedback from peers is also extremely valuable both to the person receiving the feedback and the person providing it. Learners may ask their peers for feedback naturally: for instance on an art course, a learner might ask a peer if the colour or perspective looks realistic. They can choose to accept or challenge the opinion of a peer.

The tutor can build upon this learner interaction to make peer assessment part of the course. We have already seen how groups of learners can draw up their own assessment criteria for a task, using mind-mapping software and how this can be built upon to introduce the concept of peer assessment.

The term 'Web 2.0' includes online tools which enable users to shape content and comment on each other's content. These tools allow people to share text, images and sound online easily. Using Web 2.0 tools provides ways in which learners can share their work easily and in doing so peers can assess. This can help to encourage and motivate learners as well as build up a support system for them that continues outside the classroom.

> knew the prices they went for; totally out of her league! It was like walking into OK magazine, glamorous, tasteful and truly expensive.
>
> Re: Undercover
> by Susannah - Monday, 17 September 2007, 11:12 AM
> Wow - you need to finish your story. It really is gripping stuff.. and to think it all started from an unfinished sentence. Show parent | Edit | Split | Delete | Reply
>
> Re: Undercover
> by Nina - Tuesday, 18 September 2007, 12:49 PM
> A really good development here - glad that you kept it up despite work commitments, as it's really paid off. The shift back into Serena's past is very revealing, ...

The tutor on the Isle of Wight's Fiction for Beginners course encouraged learners to use the 'Pen and Ink' forum to upload pieces of their writing on a weekly basis for other learners to read and review.

Applying effective questioning techniques and giving feedback that is more than just a grade or a score

When assessing learners' knowledge and skills we use a variety of questioning techniques. Software tools provide us with the means to replicate and extend these techniques. Closed questions can be asked using multiple-choice assessment, possibly delivered through interactive software such as 'Hot Potatoes'. Open questions can be posed through tools that allow free text answers. Software can be used to simulate situations that test a learner's ability to apply the skills they have been taught.

Katrina found that Microsoft PowerPoint had far more potential than she'd actually realised when devising assessments for learners. It enabled her ask multiple-choice questions to test knowledge, hot-spot screens to assess application of skills, and interactive text boxes to assess deeper understanding and changes in attitude.

She found it was possible to offer differentiated assessments for each learner: she built in additional support, and made them far more applicable and interesting than she had done previously simply by making use of multimedia and web links.

However, she found great care was required when writing the questions and in providing proper constructive feedback. For some questions she found the most appropriate way to feed back was in person.

Providing assessments in this way enables the tutor to offer assessments differentiated by level and by mode of testing.

The work of Black and Wiliam has shown that test scores alone produce very little improvement in future attainment, but that feedback has far greater impact. The mark will tell a learner if they have done well or not but it will not help them to see what they need to do in order to improve. When devising electronic tests, tutors must build in their own feedback to learners. It is important for the tutor to recognise that the test results and initial feedback represent a starting-point for a dialogue with the learner and that sometimes this dialogue needs to continue through email exchange or in a face-to-face meeting.

Creating a positive learning environment where learners feel relaxed

Learners need to feel relaxed if they are to concentrate well and the same applies when a learner is assessed. The way in which an assessment is delivered can have a huge impact. Technology provides alternative means of assessing learners which can remove the negative feelings learners often associate with paper-based tests.

Plymouth Adult and Community Learning Services using voting technologies in a 'Test the City' promotion.

The use of class voting handsets can provide a fun and engaging way to assess learners. These methods are used in popular television quiz programmes, so most learners find this familiar and unthreatening. Assessing by this means allows learners to see answers immediately and to talk between questions, which can help to relax them and build peer support.

Summary

The ever-expanding range of digital technologies and software applications available to teachers means that there is enormous scope to develop methods which facilitate and enhance the assessment for learning process so that it is practical and 'fit for purpose'. These digital tools can provide a means to initiate a dialogue with learners or offer them an opportunity to share their reflections in order for the tutor to build and deliver an appropriate learning programme.

Multimedia can be used to ensure that assessments are realistic and offer variety. Assessments delivered digitally can provide instant feedback and additional support for the learner. However, the process is not complete unless the results build a dialogue with learners about their learning.

3

Learning from quizzes and questions

Quizzes and tests are often used to assess progress during a course. Here we will explore the different ways that quizzes can be created and delivered through software applications and other digital technologies. For these to be part of an *assessment for learning*, detailed feedback must be given, and it does help if this feedback can be given in a variety of ways.

We will start by looking at the contexts in which quizzes may be used, then go on to look at the range of quizzes and methods of delivering them. Finally, we will look at ways of providing feedback and ways of making sure quizzes are accessible to all learners.

Quizzes in a context

Quizzes and tests provide one important way for assessing the level of understanding and progress being made on a course; other methods will be discussed in later chapters. With so many types of quizzes to choose from and many ways of delivering them, it is important to make the right choice. In order to make this choice well, it is important to understand the context in which the quiz is being used. The following questions help to understand this context.

Why use a quiz for assessment during a course?

Every session we deliver has learning outcomes, these will include those agreed for the whole group and specific outcomes for individuals. Quizzes can be a very quick and efficient way of allowing teachers and learners to measure how much learning has taken place and to inform planning for future sessions. The practical aspects of subjects such as sport, art, drama, craft and language may be better assessed through observation of a learner's performance in a skill. This will be covered in Chapter 4.

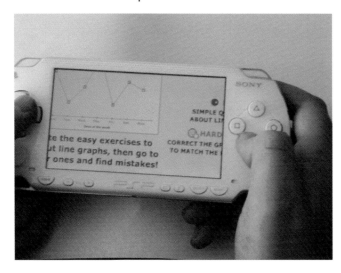

A maths quiz being taken on a PlayStation Portable (PSP).

Where will the quiz take place?

Quizzes can be set for the whole group together in the classroom or for individuals to take at their own computers, or other devices, in the classroom. They can also be taken online, at home or at work and even on location on a field trip using handheld devices. As advances in learning technology present such a variety of options, it is important to give thought to choosing the location which is most helpful to the learners. For example, some people may find that taking a quiz alone at home is less intimidating than taking it in class, but the initial feedback will be restricted to the automated responses in the software and more detailed discussions with the tutor will only follow later.

Who will be taking the quiz?

It is important to consider the needs of the learner group, including their level of ICT skills, any learning difficulties or disabilities, and any preferences they have for types of quiz.

Even when a quiz is presented in a low profile or light-hearted manner it can be a stressful and uncomfortable experience for a learner, as they can feel judged in the presence of their peers. Not all learners will view a quiz in the same way; the more confident learners may view a quiz more favourably than students who are finding the course very challenging.

Some alternatives

This part of the computer displays the software.
CTRL + click to follow link

Mouse Mat
Monitor
Keyboard
Tower Unit

A screen tip lets a learner with visual disabilities get a clue at to where the arrow was pointing

JISC TechDis

Unlocking Potential

How will feedback be given?

Frequent and thoughtful feedback is essential if assessment is to contribute to good learning. The raw scores showing the number of correct answers is the starting point but these usually show only what is fully understood and are not good indicators of what is partly understood. Good quiz software tools include automated feedback to learners; we deal with this in more detail later in this chapter.

Choosing a quiz type

Quiz questions can be set in exciting and different ways, and through the use of electronic methods familiar question types can become more interactive and new methods become available. Teachers need to develop the ability to select the best way of posing questions to test progress.

Here are some examples of ways that quiz questions can be set:

> multiple choice – select *one correct answer from a list*;
> multiple response – *select a number of correct responses from a list*;
> cloze exercises – *gap filling in sentences*;
> short answers questions – *free text answers are typed in*;
> matching – *linking words or images*;
> hot spots – *selecting areas of a digital image in response to a question*;
> sequencing – *placing images or words in a correct order*.

Software and hardware tools are available to use to set-up and run quizzes. Some are designed specifically for quizzes, others are integrated into other software such as a learning platform like Moodle. It is also possible to create quizzes using widely available software such as Microsoft® Word, PowerPoint® or Excel®.

In looking at each of these types of quiz we will also give some examples of particular software and devices which can be used. These will not be exhaustive, but a list of quiz-making tools appears in the Appendix at the end of this book.

Multiple-choice and multiple-response questions

Multiple-choice questions are a popular way of assessing learners as part of initial and formative assessment. In addition to the question itself, the learner is offered one correct answer and a number of incorrect answers or distracters. They are familiar to most learners, and if questions are well written they can be easily marked by software. However, writing good multiple-choice questions is an art to be perfected. A multiple-response question is similar to multiple-choice, except that the learner is asked to select more than one element from the list of possible answers.

Five key points in writing multiple-choice or multiple-response questions

1. **Clarity**: Avoid confusion by removing any unnecessary wording in both question and answers. Use plain English.
2. **Credibility**: Make all possible answers credible.
3. **Avoid giving away the answer:**
    Take care not to:
    - have a leading question;
    - provide the answer to one question in the body of another's question;
    - have a pattern for the position of the correct answer.
4. **Trialling**: Fully test your quiz before you use it with learners.
5. **Feedback**: Write constructive feedback for correct and incorrect answers.

Learners write their own tests

Sally Jowers at Colchester ACL asks her learners to write multiple-choice questions in groups at the end of each topic. She encourages them to make the questions 'hard'. This had a number of benefits: the learners review the topic, the learners create their own revision questions. By reviewing their questions, Sally is able to see which areas her learners thought were hard or what caused the confusion.

TIP

To improve your skills at writing multiple-choice questions try these online tutorials:

Hot Potatoes:
http://hotpot.uvic.ca/howto/mcquestion.htm

Computer Assisted Assessment Centre's Guide to Objective Tests:
www.caacentre.ac.uk/resources/index.shtml

There are many software tools and technologies to enable teachers to create and deliver multiple-choice quizzes in the most appropriate way for particular learners.

The use of hyperlinks and action buttons in PowerPoint can provide a quick and effective means of creating interactive assessments. Users have full control over the feedback given after each question. It is easy to build-in additional support for those learners who need it.

It is also possible to create multiple-choice assessments using drop-down boxes in a word-processing package such as Word or a spreadsheet such as Excel. Excel has a feature called 'IF statements' and these can be used to provide feedback.

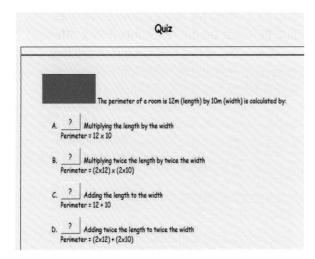

The perimeter of a room is 12m (length) by 10m (width) is calculated by:

A. ? Multiplying the length by the width
Perimeter = 12 x 10

B. ? Multiplying twice the length by twice the width
Perimeter = (2x12) x (2x10)

C. ? Adding the length to the width
Perimeter = 12 + 10

D. ? Adding twice the length to twice the width
Perimeter = (2x12) + (2x10)

A numeracy quiz created using Hot Potatoes software.

Multiple-choice and multiple-response questions always feature in special quiz software. Examples of this kind of software are 'Hot Potatoes', 'Question Tools' and the 'Quiz' feature in the Moodle learning platform. In addition to using a PC, classroom response systems provide voting handsets to all students which can be used to select answers from a class whiteboard.

A learner takes an assessment on a PC phone.

This type of quiz can also be created for mobile devices such as mobile phones, iPods and Personal Digital Assistants (PDA), offering the learner flexibility in when they assess their progress and how often they undertake that assessment. For more information on using mobile devices see e-guideline 12, *Handheld technologies for mobile learning.*

TIP

PocketExam Builder (***www.bizon.org***) and Quizzler (***www.quizzlerpro.org***) allow quizzes to be developed for handheld portable devices e.g. iPods, iPhones and PDAs.

Classroom response systems in action

The Family Learning Tutors at Portsmouth City Council use voting handsets for initial and formative assessments. They have found that this method really does enable assessment for learning – the instant information it provides can impact immediately on how they go on to plan their teaching because:

> It highlights support needs – the tutor runs a test looking at the learners' faces seeing their reaction to both questions and answers, as well as how quickly they answer each individual questions.
> It highlights the group's learning needs – from the results charts, the tutor can see how the group answers a question and can make an instant decision on how to adapt the session as a result of the information. Tutors find they can teach after each question as a need is identified, rather than leaving it for later in the session or the programme.
> It highlights individual learning needs – on seeing the results, the learners ask questions or ask for help. Tutors have found that learners made comments about not being able to do particular topics at school or when they are trying to help their child with homework. Tutors can use this as an opportunity to open up group discussions.

Source: Using voting technology for assessment, NRDC. Sally Betts and Maria Kambouri

Gap-fill or 'cloze' assessments

Gap-fill exercises – sometimes called 'cloze' – are often used in language programmes to assess a learner's reading, spelling and grammar skills. In addition to testing language skills, gap-fill exercises can be used as a framework to test factual knowledge in any area of learning. As with multiple-choice and multiple-response tests it is very important to ensure that cloze tests do not allow any ambiguity. There should be only one possible answer. It is also important that you don't create too many gaps and in doing so, make the exercise impossible to complete. It is best not to remove more than one in every eight words.

These assessments can be easily created using Word, but can also be created using most quiz software. Text messaging on a mobile phone has been used as a way of sending a single gapped sentence to learners for a response. A cloze test can also be given as part of a live online text chat session as the teacher pastes the gapped sentence into the window and students compete to be first to fill the gap.

14:58 Kate: They wanted to go to the shops, they decided to .... the bus.

14:58 Dee: is it catch?

15:00 Kate: Well done, yes you can use the word catch, it does sound a little strange, as you can't physically 'catch a bus' in the same way you can 'catch a ball'.

An ESOL tutor makes use of a chat room to deliver cloze exercises.

> **TIP**
>
> Exe Learning is free software which lets you create self-contained learning materials including quizzes which can be loaded into a virtual learning environment (VLE) or saved to a CD-ROM or USB memory stick. Materials created meets SCORM standards, which means quiz scores can be saved directly into a central student record.

Short-answer exercises

Many software applications, including Word, PowerPoint and Hot Potatoes, allow a user to enter short text answers to questions. Some software will also mark as 'correct' exact matches with the pre-loaded correct answer. This can be very useful where spelling and use of capitalisation and punctuation are being tested. However, as the software will be very pedantic, beware that very minor errors such as adding an extra space between words, could render a correct answer to be marked wrong. It is also very important to ensure that all possible alternative correct answers are acceptable.

*Family
Learning,
Portsmouth*

Short answers can also be given in spoken rather than written form. It is also possible in Word and PowerPoint presentation graphics program to allow an audio response and embed the sound file in the document.

Michelle shows her learners how to use the sound recording facility in Word to assess their language skills in French.

Matching exercises

'Drag and drop' exercises allow the learner to move items around on a screen to demonstrate their understanding of the relationships between objects, words or concepts.

This type of quiz is popular with people who find it easy to express relationships using pictures and diagrams.

Hot Potatoes and Picture Grid Editor provide two simple tools to create matching exercises. These can be delivered using an interactive whiteboard or a PC.

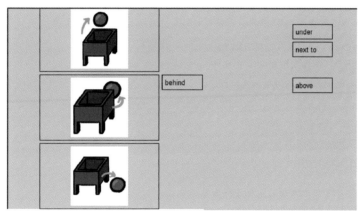

Positional vocabulary drag and drop exercise created in Hot Potatoes. It makes use of the image library on the Hot Potatoes website.

TIP

The Hot Potatoes website provides an image library. The images are in the correct format to upload straight into a Hot Potatoes quiz.
http://hcmc.uvic.ca/clipart/

Hot spot exercises

In a hot spot exercise, a learner uses a computer mouse to select a point on a screen image to indicate a correct answer. The use of an image can itself be more engaging than text as the image can represent a real work scenario, for instance health and safety hazards in the workplace

This technique can be flexible and offer a creative way of presenting a quiz. Hot spots are placed in an image by creating transparent textboxes which are hyperlinked to the relevant response, either <correct> or <incorrect>.

Kathy Cockcroft, IT Tutor, has found that hot spots in PowerPoint are a fun way to access a learner's IT skills especially on basic IT courses.

Kathy also uses the hot spot method to ensure learners know what each of the icons on a toolbar do.

*Study where the cursor is positioned in the word below. You need to delete **super** from the word supermarket. Which key would you press to delete each letter*

super|market

The backspace delete key has a hotspot over it which links to the correct answer feedback. All other keys are linked to the feedback for an incorrect answer.

Sequencing

Sequencing exercises ask the learners to place items in the correct order. Many tasks that we teach our learners involve following a sequence, for example building a wall, cooking or making a découpage card. It could be possible to re-use photographs from instructional handouts and include them is a sequencing exercise. If PowerPoint Slide Sorter View or Microsoft Photo Story are used, the learners can add captions and audio to explain the process and describe why each action is necessary.

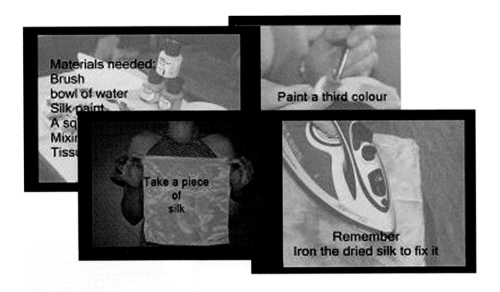

Julie Cull, Visual Arts Tutor, uses Microsoft Photo Story.

Providing feedback

'Critical in all assessments is the quality of the feedback'
Alistair McNaught, Techdis

As we have seen, the research activity in this area has shown that the quality of feedback is a crucial factor in the assessment if it is to lead to improved achievement. Feedback from quizzes can be provided automatically and instantly by the software. More detailed and personalised feedback can follow in a conversation between tutor and learner. It is important to build on automated feedback by providing a more personalised feedback to individuals based on the results of the assessment.

Feedback can tell the learner:

> whether their answer is right or wrong;
> the correct answer and explain why it is correct, thus providing a learning opportunity to consolidate learning;
> why they might have chosen their incorrect answer, helping to remove any misconceptions;
> how they could improve their work in the future;
> where they can do further learning on a topic;
> where they can get additional support.

It is possible to build many of these features into e-assessments using the software tools described in this section. However, to have the greatest impact on learning, the assessment should lead to a dialogue between tutor and learner in order to ensure that future learning needs are identified and so that forward plans can take account of them.

Good feedback provides additional benefits – sometimes described as 'softer outcomes':

> it can build a person's self-confidence;
> it can help the learner to become better at recognising their strengths and weaknesses;

> It can help to build a trusting relationship between tutor and learner;

> it can foster peer support.

TIP

Chat facilities with webcams can provide 1:1 feedback opportunities with all the advantages of being carried out in a face-to-face tutorial, such as being able to read body language, but with the additional benefits of being held at convenient times and in privacy – not always possible in a class of 16.

TIPS TO GIVING FEEDBACK

'If you're giving feedback online then it needs to be given frequently, it needs to be timely and you need to use all the communication methods available to you.'

'Be honest, learners appreciate that.'

Terry Loane

'Feedback is a three-way process, tutor to learner, learner to tutor and learners to learners.'

Judith Gawn NIACE

Ensuring that quizzes are accessible to all

We all have a legal responsibility to make sure that our assessments, just like the learning materials we create, are accessible to all. So in creating e-assessments, it is essential to consider each learner's individual needs and make reasonable adjustments if necessary. Special devices and software can provide a way to make simple changes to existing assessments or offer an alternative method of assessing, although care needs to be taken to ensure they are comparable.

'Accessibility is about removing barriers to participation and engagement.'

Techdis

Not all software applications or technologies are accessible to all users, but often small changes can make an assessment more widely accessible. A change which helps improve accessibility for learners with a particular need can often benefit all users.

Some examples of accessibility adjustments

> Providing audio questions for learners with low literacy levels or dyslexia.
> Providing a tactile set of photographs for a sequencing activity.
> Providing "drag and drop" exercises on an interactive whiteboard rather than a computer screen for learners with poor motor skills.
> Using the 'Text to Speech' toolbar in Excel (2002) to read the words in a cloze exercise for learners with visual impairments.

TIP

The Techdis e-assessment staff pack gives more information about making assessments accessible.
www.techdis.ac.uk/resources/sites/staffpacks

Summary

The use of digital technology to create and deliver quizzes can play an important part in assessment to improve learning. They can be flexible and engaging but an essential element is the quality of the feedback that they offer.

Electronic quizzes can:

> be less daunting for the learner than paper-based methods;
> provide the tutor with instant information that they can then use to inform teaching;

> provide the learner with instant feedback that their tutor has written and direct access to further support materials;
> reduce marking time and provide easy ways to store results.

Time is needed to learn new software and to build confidence in using technologies but the benefits in doing so can be substantial.

Using quizzes is not the only way in which learners can be assessed. In the next chapter we will look at the recording of practical skills as a starting point in an assessment process.

4

Recording what learners do and what they create

The previous chapter looked at the way that quizzes can contribute to assessment for learning. While quizzes use questions and exercises to test specific knowledge and understanding, this chapter focuses on ways of capturing evidence of learners making progress in performing the skills that they have signed-up to learn. We now have many inexpensive devices, which can help us to record sound, still images, moving images and text. This chapter will explore how their use can be integrated into learning programmes to enrich assessment which involves both teachers and learners. We will look at practical issues associated with collecting, storing and presenting the digital evidence to allow learners to track their own progress and to stimulate their reflection which we will discuss further in Chapter 5.

Capturing performance

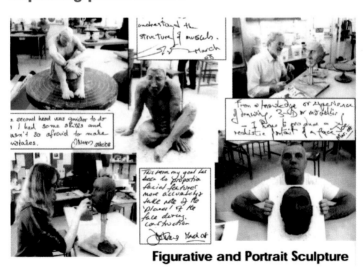

Figurative and Portrait Sculpture

This can play a very important part of continuous on-course assessment. We have already recognised, in Chapter 2, the importance to assessment for learning of a positive learning environment where learners feel relaxed. It is important not to compromise this when recordings are made of learners. The teacher will need to make a professional judgement as to how soon in a course learners will be ready for the performance of a skill to be observed and captured. For example, in a badminton course it may be very helpful as part of initial assessment to take a video of a learner's serving technique in order to analyse faults. In contrast, asking a new beginner in French to be recorded at the start of a course trying to struggle through reading a sentence in an unfamiliar language could just be humiliating and demotivating.

However, once a course has started, all learners will be developing skills and using their new knowledge and their performance can be observed and samples recorded. It is important to be mindful of the importance of feedback from teacher and peers so, however the recording is made, there should be facilities for easy playback, and time set aside for review and discussion. Learners and teacher then need to use the review to plan the next stage of the learning.

We can now choose from a wide range of digital methods to do this. However, the key element of success is to make sure that the methods used are not intrusive. Any recording should be in the control of the learners who should have easy access but should also be able to determine who else can see the material.

Most physical skills can be observed and reviewed very well using a video camera. A conventional camcorder can capture large scale action such as sports skills or dance performance. More intricate skills such as cookery techniques or craft work can be captured by a webcam or the recording facility in a special projector called a visualiser.

A visualiser, also referred to as a digital presenter acts as both a computer and a projector to enlarge the view of an intricate skill being performed for a whole class to view (it can also make a recording).

Audio recording can be a very useful way of monitoring progress in musical skills or oral ability. For language learners, improvements in accent and fluency can be monitored, but audio recordings can provide evidence of a whole range of interpersonal skills, including parenting and customer care. Another valuable use of audio recordings can be to track learner's ability to explain key concepts and they can provide a valuable focus for peer assessments.

Music

At the start of each week's guitar class Roger, the tutor, asked the learners to play the piece they have been practising at home. He found that when learners had finished playing they would often say that they had played much better at home! So he encouraged learners to record themselves at home: some accepted the challenge. At the start of each lesson they listen to the recording together and Roger pauses the track to highlight when things were played well or when there were areas for improvement.

Recording the same tune a few weeks later he finds that improvements are easily identifiable. With learner's permission he places short sound clips on the course section of the learning platform.

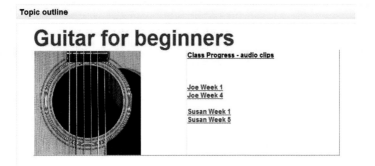

Topic outline

Guitar for beginners

Class Progress - audio clips

Joe Week 1
Joe Week 4

Susan Week 1
Susan Week 5

Reading to children

Ayesha teaches a family learning course where she asks parents and carers to record themselves reading a story to their children at home. The ability to read confidently and well is an important aspect of the course.

Through this activity, Ayesha was able to hear how skills covered in the course were put in to practice at home. She could hear how the book was introduced, how it was read, how it was discussed and how children's questions were answered. Course participants were able to comment on their own reading.

At first the parents were a bit self-conscious but this disappeared as the recording became a familiar weekly activity. By the end of the course, the students agreed to have recordings played to the whole group.

Still images alone can sometimes provide evidence of an achievement of a created artefact (for example a piece of artwork or a cookery creation). However, images are often greatly enhanced when linked to an audio or text description by the learners of how the artefact was produced. An image can be very useful in stimulating learners to undertake the reflection that we discuss in Chapter 5.

A learner records her thoughts to images imported into Microsoft® Photo Story.

Video recording is used by Kingston ACL to assess learners on tennis courses. The video is played back to learners in order to point out areas for improvement and to help to identify the progress. Judy Evans, Curriculum Manager, explained that it was good to 'freeze frame' the video in order to highlight things such as position of arms during a service.

The main challenges were videoing a fast-moving game, editing the video files and storing the results.

With students learning ICT skills, it is possible to use software to record in real time the activity on the PC screen. This technique is called 'moving screen capture' and will record mouse movements and keyboard inputs to create a video record. This can be a good way of enabling a learner to review how she or he is using a particular software application and note ways in which this could be done more efficiently.

ICT tutors at Hillingdon Adult Education investigated using two pieces of software to capture screen movements. They used Wink and CamStudio to produce short 'how to' video demonstrations of IT applications. In this process they realised their learners could also use the software to record themselves in order to identify their own faults and put them right.

It is important if capturing an image, audio or video recording of the learner that you have the learner's agreement to do so and the learner knows exactly what you intend to do with it. The learner may agree to some or all of these uses:

> storage for review by learner and tutor alone;
> storage for review by whole class;
> storage as evidence for extended summative assessment;
> use in publicity materials available to the public.

Art

A fine arts tutor uses a digital camera to take high-quality photographs of his learners' artwork. Previously he had to take artwork away from his learners in order to get it photocopied between sessions for evidence of progression and achievement. Learners didn't mind this quite as much once the work was complete but often wanted to continue working on an unfinished sketch between sessions. He found taking the photograph had other advantages:

> he didn't need to take the artwork away;
> on seeing the picture he'd be reminded of the feedback he'd given orally during the session;
> he could bring the picture into a Word document and annotate it with the feedback;
> he could provide a copy of the Word document to the learner, which helped them to remember the points he'd made and to reflect on all the feedback he'd given – not just those points they'd remembered;
> he had evidence of progress and achievement.

The only challenge was to learn how to bring a photograph into Word and to annotate it using text boxes and arrows.

A visual arts tutor uses digital photographs to record learners' achievement in creating picture frames. On completion of their frame she takes a photo of each learner holding their frame up so that it frames their face. She finds this is an excellent way to remember whose frame was whose and to make a celebration of achievement display at the end of a course.

Although most of the learners find this a fun activity, not all are happy to have their photograph taken. As a result she now offers them the choice of being photographed in their frame or not.

Sheila Dodds' learners celebrate their achievement in their drawing and arts classes by displaying photographs of their achievement online.

Inspection evidence

As technology is introduced into our teaching practice, the validity of digital evidence is sometimes questioned, and people unfamiliar with digital techniques sometimes prefer the familiarity of paper-based approaches. Just as learners are using evidence of their progress in a range of new formats, external inspectors should also accept digital evidence so long as it can be shown to demonstrate progress and to be in a format actually useful to the learners.

'I think tutors should now have the right to expect that inspectors are able to use and access digital materials to see the evidence produced by learners and tutors in the form in which it was produced. The key to this will be in the planning stage where the nominee can insist that the inspectors are "fit for purpose" as Ofsted recognises the importance of ICT and e-learning'

Nigel Ecclesfield, (E-Moot)

'If a tutor undertakes formative assessment using digital technologies then my advice to them would be to ensure that they have documented, in their session plan, that they intend to assess in that way and the purpose of the assessment. They should also make it clear in the session evaluation how and why they will be changing future sessions as a result of undertaking that assessment.'

Steve Glennon, Quality and Curriculum Manager,
Portsmouth City Council

'My advice would be to store representative samples and not clips lasting more than a few minutes and certainly not to store everything. For me, good evidence of learning would be an agreed clip jointly identified by tutor and learner showing the achievement or development of a skill in progress. Technically I would also suggest that tutors become familiar with using quite high levels of compression as the evidence rarely needs to be of the highest quality.'

Nigel Ecclesfield (E-Moot)

Making it work – finding solutions

Capturing and managing diverse data can be challenging. It is the responsibility of the professional tutor to make judgements on the suitability of any particular method and to plan how it will fit within a pedagogical programme of activities. This will involve practical issues of equipment provision, staff and learner training, and the crucial question of acceptability to learners of any data capture. Within the complexity of technical requirements and logistics it is important that the decisions are driven by a clear understanding of what will be most effective in helping teachers and learners understand how much they have learned and how best to move forward to the next stage of learning.

This section looks at some of the practical challenges which teachers have encountered and it explores some possible solutions.

Challenge 1: Learners are not comfortable with being recorded (audio, video or photograph)

Try the following:

> Explain the purpose and the benefits to the group.
> Tell them who is going to listen/watch the recording and how long you will keep it.
> Invite learners to use the equipment to take the photographs, or make the recordings.
> Make it clear that learners have the right to accept or reject a recording or image.
> Take pictures/video so that you do not include the learner's face – show their hands performing a task, record only the product not the person.

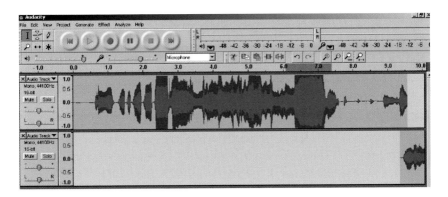

Audacity is open source software that allows you to edit sound files. Other editing software is available free or at low cost for use with video such as Windows Moviemaker.

Challenge 2: You are recording too much information

Try the following:

> Buy devices that have a pause button. This will allow the learner to talk but you only need to capture the appropriate passages. [Note: this only works if you have control of the recording device.]

> Have a general discussion around the assessment before you record. During the discussion make a comment each time the learner says something you'd like to capture. The learner is then more likely to repeat the desired responses when you ask the appropriate questions in the recording session.

> Use editing software to remove unwanted material.

Challenge 3: Running out of storage space

Try the following:

> When using the 'Sound recorder' application in Windows you can reduce the size of the file it produces. Look at the File>Properties option.

> Use audio editing software like Audacity to remove unwanted content. The sound can be saved as an MP3 file which is a compressed format, so requires less space.

> In Windows Movie Maker an imported movie can be edited to remove unwanted content but it can also be reduced in size when saving it to back to your computer. First save the file with a different name in order to keep the original. Then select the 'Best fit to file size' option and reduce the size of the output file to the lowest level that still retains the quality required.

> Remove the sound track from a video if it is not needed: this will reduce the file size. This may be good for a video of sports skills. Virtualdub software (**www.virtualdub.org**) will enable you to do this.

> Don't save the whole video but edit, using software such as Windows Movie Maker to capture images from it.

> Purchase portable external hard drive space (now reasonably low cost).

> **TIP**
>
> For more information on reducing audio and video files try a Google search for 'reducing video file sizes'.

Challenge 4: Capturing the action

Try the following:

> To capture people's positions in a game such as tennis it is not necessary to have close-up shots. Place the video camera on a tripod in a position where the whole court can be seen.
> To capture an individual's actions, only focus on that individual but ensure that you can see enough of the surroundings to cover the action that is about to take place. For instance have space above their head in your viewfinder if the learner is about to serve in tennis.

Challenge 5: Learners not having digital recording equipment

Try the following:

> Check to see if the learner has a mobile phone, camera or MP3 player. If they do, then ask them to explore the audio recording options, or see if they could use the video option on a digital still camera (for either sound or video). Many devices have functions of which we are not aware.
> Ask learners to find out if anyone in their family has equipment that could be borrowed.
> Purchase low-cost MP3 players with a voice recorder and loan them to learners.
> Purchase low-cost video cameras (e.g. Busbi and Disgo) and loan them to learners.

Challenge 6: Tutors not having the skills required

Try the following:

> Online tutorials and guidance notes on how to perform tasks are available online. Try NIACE's Staff development e-learning centre (SDELC) **www.sdelc.co.uk**
> Join technology/VLE forums online, you can post questions to other tutors who may be able to help. The Regional Development Centres run by JISC oversee a number of discussion forums.
> Find out if your organisation has an E-Guide or another tutor with skills who can support you.

Challenge 7: Learner not having the skills to use digital technologies and software

Encourage learners to use technology themselves to support their learning by providing audio/video recorded materials that they will find useful on CD, YouTube or a learning platform. Learners will become more confident in using equipment to record themselves if they also using it to access learning materials like:

> instructions for yoga or Tai Chi;
> steps for ballroom dancing;
> instructions for cooking a recipe;
> recorded vocabulary lists in language classes (try recording straight onto their mobile phone).

Summary

Observing and recording learners performing skills can provide important source of assessment data for both learner and teacher. In tracking a learner's progress and achievement teachers can draw on the collection of evidence in a range of formats.

Methods using digital technologies can play a very valuable contribution to this, and are especially important for those courses which require practical skills development. Effective teaching practice will include making sure that all the principles of good assessment are observed and that any evidence collected is made available to the learner throughout the course in appropriate ways to support them in monitoring their own progress and in helping them to recognise how they learn.

There are always challenges when introducing the use of new methods, and when technology is used with these methods there can be additional demands. The guiding principle is that the method used should be fit for the purpose of applying good assessment for learning and thus encouraging feedback and dialogue. Staff and learners should be familiar and comfortable with the equipment and software used. Above all, the benefits of using a particular method must always outweigh the effort required to use it!

5

Reflections and self-assessment

In the last two chapters we have looked at how learners and tutors can assess progress in learning through, testing knowledge and skills with tools such as quizzes and by observing performance in a task or by examining a final product.

The importance of 'providing opportunities for learners to reflect' was highlighted by the Improving Formative Assessment project as one of the six key actions for teachers (see Chapter 2). This chapter looks at the contribution to assessment that is made by learners speaking or writing about their learning. This self-assessment will include a reflection on what has been learned but also how it was learned and this process that leads to setting new learning goals for the future.

The importance of reflection in the learning cycle is also recognised in David Kolb's Learning Cycle model.

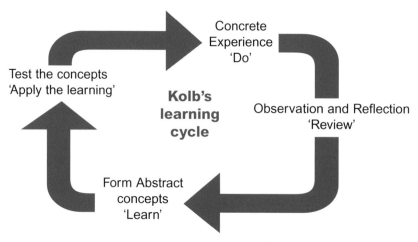

David Kolb's Learning Cycle model (from Kolb and Fry, 1975).

Kolb's model of learning shows that by having practical experience (by doing) and analysing what we are learning (thinking and reflecting on) we will understand and, in turn, take our learning forward. Reflection and discussion play key roles in raising the level of understanding.

A very useful way to initiate reflection is to invite learners to use a simple, colour-coded self-assessment. For an area of work learners can make judgements about their level of confidence in a topic.

> Green: I am fully confident with this topic;
> Amber: I am not fully confident with this topic but need more work;
> Red: I am not at all confident with this topic.

Handheld voting pads in a classroom system can be used for a whole class to vote red, amber or green giving the teacher immediate feedback. The teacher can then choose how to present the results and group learners. This could involve learners at the same level offering mutual support or could involve pairing learners at different levels.

By adding these questions to the assessment process, both learner and teacher are given another layer of information over and above test scores and observation of performance.

Tutors make time available for reflection within classes but it is a process that many learners do not find easy and if not introduced well it can be misunderstood as a distraction from the learning. It is therefore important that tutors can find ways that will enable their learners to see the true value of reflecting on their learning experience and to use a method that will fit into the learning cycle in a meaningful way.

The word, 'reflect' can be unfamiliar to many learners. How often in our normal daily lives do we take time out and reflect? Not very often, perhaps at the beginning of a new year or a key life changes – leaving school, career changes, marriage, bereavement or starting a family. In these examples we look at the broad picture of our lives, but consciously reflecting on small aspects of an activity such as learning a skill may be unfamiliar to many learners.

TIP

The Individual Learning Plan can be a simple word-processed document that both learner and tutor update and review on a regular basis. To provide the opportunity to share the document online easily try Google Docs.

Another way to achieve a shared ILP could be through the use of a Wiki, where different people can read and edit the single document.

Models of reflection

Reflecting on a learner's own ability starts from the moment that he or she considers joining a class. As part of initial assessment the learning provider will ask a learner:

1 What do you already know?
2 What do you want to know and why?

From this the provider can start to plan a way for a learner to achieve his or her aims.

This often becomes part of a learner's Individual Learning Plan (ILP) or Learning Record and is used to track a learner's progress through the course.

Having a framework for posing questions can be helpful to learners who find reflection unfamiliar. Here are two possible frameworks from which key questions can be derived.

The Generic Learning Outcomes (GLO) model

In order to make reflection meaningful, many learners require some guidance. The Inspiring Learning for All Framework (**www.inspiringlearningforall.gov.uk**) provides a model for measuring progress against learning outcomes, one that tutors can implement on a weekly basis.

The Generic Learning Outcomes (GLO) Model – a framework for regular reflection

Using these headings together with a series of detailed questions, the learners are helped to focus not just on the knowledge and skills they have acquired but also on the value these will have and how they can be put into practice.

> **TIP**
>
> Create a template for a reflective diary for learners with a picture of the GLO model and accompany it with more detailed questions, e.g. 'Do you feel more confident about using..?' 'How will you use what you have learnt in this session?' The reflective diary could be in the form of a blog or an online journal. Many VLEs have these inbuilt functions.

Reflective Questions – Helen Barrett

Dr Helen Barrett suggests reflection can be encouraged and shaped by means of three broad questions that link past learning to future plans for learning. This is a framework for reflecting as a learner reaches a 'milestone' on the learning journey – an end-of-section or mid-term review. (See Helen Barrett **http://electronicportfolios.org**)

These questions are: 'What?' 'So what?' and 'What next?'

> 'What?'

 The answer to this question will be a description of what has been learned and a summary of the evidence of learning. This could be scores in tests and quizzes, as discussed in Chapter 3, but it is also likely to include evidence of learning in the form of the type of artefact or performance that we discussed in Chapter 4.

> 'So what?'

 The answer to this question will be the reflection on what has been learned so far – so it will offer a self-assessment of progress and also some thoughts on how the learning took place.

> What next?

 The answer to this takes the learner into the section of the Kolb's learning cycle where learning will be applied and tested and, possibly, new learning goals set.

At the milestone point where these three questions are posed, the learner will need to have access to the results of earlier work (quiz scores and evidence of performance), a space to reflect and a space to set new goals. We will say more about managing this information in the final chapter.

Structured conversations in health and fitness

Judy Evans is Curriculum Manager at Kingston ACL where she encourages tutors to hold conversations with learners for the initial and formative assessment in keep fit, yoga, pilates and Tai Chi classes.

Although these are conducted as conversations, the tutor uses a list of key questions to ensure that the initial assessment is completed by asking about learners' previous experience and reasons for taking the class. The conversations are saved by a small digital voice recorder and used by the tutor to plan the course sessions.

Four weeks into the course, the tutors hold a further recorded conversation with learners to assess progress. This includes asking how the learner feels they are doing and asking them to identify areas they feel they need more work.

Catching reflections

A learning log or diary is often used to collect reflections. This can be placed online as a blog (weblog) and may be incorporated into a learning platform. Learners will often be anxious or concerned about access to these logs. The learner will need to feel in control. Initially, access may only be granted to the learner and tutor but, as trust develops in a group, settings can be changed and fellow-learners invited to view each other's contributions and offer comment. The introduction of peer contributions to assessment of progress can provide added richness to the dialogue.

Of course, reflection can also be provided in an audio recording or on video. One learning provider used the idea of the 'Big Brother' Diary Room. At the end of each session, each learner had time in the Diary Room, reflecting on what they had learned in a private room in front of a video camera.

Video can provide a rich record including, as it does, facial expression and body language. However, it can be daunting. Audio recordings are regarded by some people as much less intrusive than video and they can be made with equipment which is less costly and easier to set up. Here is a good example of a case where a teacher should use his or her understanding of the learner group and the subject matter to make a professional judgement over the best method to use.

Preparing questions

In capturing spoken reflections, the tutor can pose key questions. Open questions should be used and prepared in advance including possible supplementary questions.

If the activity is well prepared, the task of asking the questions can be passed to other learners so that the group members take turns to interview each other. For this to work there will need to be a degree of trust within the group and a clear set of expectations. Questions can be provided on paper, but the results of one action research project using this system showed that learners conducted interviews best after they had watched someone else conduct an interview.

Linking artefacts

A key element of any reflection will be the link to evidence of achievement collected so far in the course. For example an audio interview could include inviting learners to comment on images of past course achievement, or a learners could be asked to include in blog a comment on a printout of their quiz scores.

Summary

Reflecting on learning is a key part of the learning process and one that learners can find hard to undertake. Also, they may not immediately see the reason for it. Technology can be used effectively to allow learners to reflect at times that suit them, not just within the confines of the classroom. By encouraging and fostering reflective practice with learners, teachers can lead learners to take on ownership and management of their learning.

Audio reflections can have a strong impact, as the learners' own voice adds an additional layer of emotion to the words.

Evidence of learners' performance in a course presents the raw material for reflection. Hence, it is important that systems are set up to enable learners to keep together the artefacts they collect throughout their learning so that they can be linked to their reflections. The next chapter will explore how this can be achieved where the process of *assessment for learning* can be supported by a *portfolio for learning*.

6

e-portfolios for learning

In this book we have seen the way in which the quality of a learning experience can be enhanced through the tutor–learner dialogue based on assessment evidence. That assessment evidence can include results of quizzes and tests, the observation of a learner's performance or learners' self-assessment through reflection of their progress. This chapter will look at how a digital record of a learning journey can be used to draw together the story of that journey. The application of *assessment for learning* will be integral to that story.

Categories of e-portfolio

The term e-portfolio is often used to describe the drawing together of digital artefacts in one place to document a learner's journey. However, the term can also be used to describe digital archives with quite different purposes, and this can cause confusion. For example, the secure online space for storing and marking summative assessments is sometimes described as an e-portfolio, as are collections of evidence destined for external verifiers as part of final assessment. The term e-portfolio is also used to describe an electronic showcase of achievement, which may be used as part of a job application process, and, finally, the term can be used for a space to support career development.

However, in the context of *assessment for learning* an e-portfolio represents the digital archive used by learner and tutor to store and manage the process of using assessment to improve the learning process.

In summary, e-portfolios are usually seen as having four possible functions:

> portfolio for summative assessment;
> portfolio for presentation or showcasing;
> portfolio for career development and progression;
> portfolio for learning, including assessment for learning.

(List adapted from documents produced by: Centre for Recording Achievement and British Educational Communication Technology Agency.)

Although these functions need not be mutually exclusive, and it is possible to combine functions within a single portfolio, there can be confusion over the purpose and audience for a particular entry. Some have argued, in particular, that a *portfolio for learning* is best kept quite separate from a *portfolio for assessment*. The *assessment for learning* portfolio may contain 'work in progress' and sensitive reflection that helps the learning process but which the learner may not wish to have shared with people responsible for external assessment.

In practice, an *assessment portfolio* may contain a selection of the content in the *portfolio for learning*. It is, however, important that tutors and learners are clear about the purpose of any portfolio entry and the audience for that entry.

e-portfolios for learning

It is the *portfolio for learning* that will contain artefacts that support assessment for learning, so in this chapter we will focus solely on this function of a portfolio. This type of portfolio could be based on an Individual Learning Plan and would contain artefacts produced by all the activities so far discussed in this book.

Drawing together the digital artefacts of the learning journey

Specialist software systems have been created to provide e-portfolios. Some of these are commercial products for which licence fees must be paid, but for others, open source software is available at no cost. There are also e-portfolio systems which are designed to integrate into other software, for instance there are several e-portfolio systems which can integrate with the Moodle learning platform. However, a portfolio can be created simply by using an electronic document folder on a shared network or by placing files on a portable memory stick.

The guiding principle is that the portfolio should enable the learner to collect together and then access the artefacts of the learning journey. The portfolio will hold the materials and results of the *assessment for learning* process and will be designed to enhance the tutor–learner dialogue.

A good *portfolio for learning* structure will present opportunities to contain and display evidence of all aspects of the assessment that has taken place during a learning journey. This will include results of tests, evidence of performance and reflection.

The structure of the *portfolio for learning* should lead the learner from what has been achieved to a reflection and then set future goals. Dr Helen Barratt's three key questions, 'What?', 'So what?' and 'What next?' (see Chapter 5) can be helpful way of structuring a portfolio.

The portfolio should:

> be easily accessible by learners;
> give equal weight to electronic artefacts in any format;
> be secure and in the control of the learner.

Creating the e-portfolio for learning

The process of portfolio collection and presentation is paramount. As we said earlier in this chapter, there are many technical ways of producing a portfolio for learning; the solution that is adopted should reflect the available resources and the ICT skill level of learner and tutor. However, above all the system should be designed to support the dialogue between learner and tutor. It should help the learner by giving easy access to the digital artefacts.

Simple start

Many tutors using a portfolio for learning approach for the first time have found it useful to start with the simplest and most familiar technology. A popular starting portfolio can be created using a folder on a shared drive or a portable pen drive. The portfolio framework can be created on a single-page Word document following the pattern of:

> What we did;
> What we learned;
> What we will do next.

Hyperlinks can then be created to the files that illustrate the process. A Word document saved on a memory stick gives a summary of the

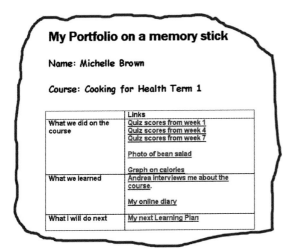

My Portfolio on a memory stick

Name: Michelle Brown

Course: Cooking for Health Term 1

	Links
What we did on the course	Quiz scores from week 1 Quiz scores from week 4 Quiz scores from week 7 Photo of bean salad Graph on calories
What we learned	Andrea interviews me about the course. My online diary
What I will do next	My next Learning Plan

learning journey and has hyperlinks to additional sources of evidence and reflection.

In a similar way, a template can be set up in PowerPoint offering the key headings; then images, text, video and audio files can all be embedded or hyperlinked.

Dr Helen Barrett has been researching strategies and technologies for e-portfolios since 1991 and is an advocate of simple systems. She has demonstrated how familiar tools can be used to create portfolios for learning by producing 34 versions of her own e-portfolio using different tools, including many free online Web 2.0 applications such as Google Docs.

Summary

An e-portfolio for learning is a digital space which can be online or offline. It will be set up specifically to draw together the digital elements of a learning journey and allow the learner and tutor to access these as part of their ongoing dialogue.

e-portfolios may also be created for summative assessment, to provide a presentation or showcases space or to support career progression. Where a portfolio has more than one function, it is important to be clear about the purpose and the audience for every digital element within the portfolio.

7
Conclusion

'Assessment for learning' is used to provide an understanding of how the learner is progressing so that both learner and teacher can modify future learning activities to maximise achievement. This understanding will grow from informed dialogue between the two, and the learner will use this understanding to take more control of his or her learning. Meanwhile, the teacher will use this understanding to adapt the teaching programme.

There is a large range of digital methods available to support assessment for learning and these methods can produce evidence and data in a myriad of ways. The challenge for those involved in teaching is to select appropriate methods and harness these to enrich the discussions between teacher and learner.

We have seen that, in addition to promoting dialogue, good assessment for learning will also encourage learners to draw up their own assessment criteria and to reflect on their learning. It will also enable students to assess each other and ensure that teachers provide detailed and constructive feedback. These are all recommendations of the Improving Formative Assessment project which has also indicated the great importance of 'creating a positive learning environment where learners feel relaxed'. We should be mindful of this whenever we use learning technologies to implement assessment for learning and take care to select digital methods, which will contribute to that positive and relaxed environment.

8

Glossary

Audacity	Free online software that allows you to capture, edit and re-format audio files.
blog	An online journal, also referred to as a web log.
closed questions	Questions that restrict the number of possible answers, such as questions that only allow the answers 'yes' or 'no'.
CD-ROM	A computer data storage device.
class response system	A system which uses wireless connected handsets to allow learners in a class to respond to questions displayed on the whiteboard and record their responses.
e-portfolio	Digital storage spaces allowing learners to make an electronic record of their work, progress and achievements.
Google	A popular search engine.
Google Docs	Free web-based tools including a word processor that allows you to create collaborative documents.
handheld devices	Portable technologies such as PDAs, MP3 players that can be used in teaching and learning.
hyperlink	A link that takes you to another location or resource used a lot to link Internet pages but can be used within MS Office applications.

ICT	Information Communication Technology. Technology incorporating computers and networking.
ILP	Individual Learning Plan. A learning plan used with learners to document their learning needs and progress.
Internet	The worldwide network of computers.
iPod	Apple's digital audio player.
iPhone	Apple's internet enabled mobile phone.
IT	Information Technology.
learning platform	An online location where the learner's electronic learning resources can be accessed and organised. Sometimes referred to as a Virtual Learning Environment (VLE).
mind mapping	A visual representation of ideas or thoughts that are linked.
MP3	MPEG Audio Layer 3 – a common file format for music and other audio content.
Memory Stick	A portable data-storage device used with technology such as computers, digital projectors. 'Memory Stick' is a proprietary name; the general name is 'flash drive'.
MP3 player	A digital audio player.
multimedia	Used to describe the inclusion of graphics, sound and videos to enhance learning materials.
NVQ	National Vocational Qualification.
open questions	Questions that encourage longer answers, the opposite of a closed question.
open source software	Software which is made available free of charge, with free access to the source code.

PDA	Personal Digital Assistant.
visualiser	Also known as a digital presenter, they project documents or objects via a digital projector. Allows close-up viewing of small items, e.g. performing a cross-stitch.
VLE	Virtual Learning Environment – see learning platform.
voting technologies	See class response system.
Web 2.0	Term used to describe the trend of the online World Wide Web and web design to enhance information-sharing and collaboration amongst users. It includes online tools which allow users to contribute content and comment on content contributed by others. It includes social networking tools such as blogs and wikis.
web cams	Small digital cameras that connect to a computer and allow video to be captured or other Internet users to see via the camera.
wiki	A software tool which allows users to collaborate on the creation and editing of a document.
Wikipedia	A free online encyclopaedia created using wiki software to enable Internet users to contribute to its content.
Youtube	A free online video-sharing web site.

9
References and further reading

Assessment Reform Group (ARG) (1999) *Assessment for Learning –
Beyond the black box.* Available for download from
http://k1.ioe.ac.uk/tlrp/arg/AssessInsides.pdf .

Assessment Reform Group (ARG) (2002) 'Assessment for Learning 10
Principles'. Research-based principles to guide classroom practice.
Available for download from http://k1.ioe.ac.uk/tlrp/arg/CIE3.PDF.

Assessment Reform Group (ARG) (2002) *Testing, Motivation and
Learning.* Available for download from
http://k1.ioe.ac.uk/tlrp/arg/TML%20BOOKLET%20complete.pdf .

Barrett, H. *White Paper: The Reflect Initiative, Researching Electronic
Portfolios and Learner Achievement* –Available for download from
http://electronicportfolios.org/reflect/whitepaper.pdf .

CRA (The Centre for Recording Achievement). *e-portfolios.*
www.recordingachievement.org/eportfolios/default.asp .

Betts, S. and Kambouri, M. (2007*), Using voting technology for
assessment.* London: NRDC.

Black, P. and Wiliam, D. (1998) *Raising standards through classroom
assessment.* London: nfer Nelson.

Black, P., Harrison, C., Lee, C., Marshall, B. and Wiliam, D. (2004)
Working inside the black box, Assessment for learning the classroom.
London: nfer Nelson.

Black, P., Harrison, C., Lee, C., Marshall, B. and Wiliam, D. (2003)
Assessment for Learning: Putting It into Practice. Stony Stratford:
Open University Press.

Clark, A. and Hussain-Ahmed, S. (2006) *Signalling Success: Paper-free
approaches to recognising and recording learner progress and
achievement.* Leicester: NIACE. More information and ordering
details: www.niace.org.uk/publications/S/signalling.asp .

Dawson, D. (2007) *Handheld technologies for mobile learning*. Leicester: NIACE. More information and ordering details: www.niace.org.uk/publications/H/handheld.asp .

Improving Formative Assessment (IFA) (2002). A research project, funded by the Nuffield Foundation, NRDC and QIA, working in partnership with the Oxford-Brookes University, the University of Exeter, the University of Brighton, LSN and NIACE. The project draws on the work of Black and Wiliam in secondary schools (see above). Led by Kathryn Ecclestone at Oxford Brookes University. www.brookes.ac.uk/schools/education/staffinfo/eccleston-FAproject.html .

JISC (2005) *Innovative Practice with e-learning*. Available for download from www.jisc.ac.uk/eli_practice.html

JISC (2007) Effective Practice with e-assessment. Available for download from www.jisc.ac.uk/publications/publications/pub_eassesspracticeguide .aspx

JISC TechDis. *e-assessment Staff Pack*, Available for download from www.techdis.ac.uk/resources/sites/staffpacks/index.xml (e-assessment on menu bar)

Kolb, D. A. and Fry, R. (1975) 'Toward an applied theory of experiential learning', in C. Cooper (ed.) *Theories of Group Process*. London: John Wiley

Mellar, H., Kambouri, M., Logan, K., Betts, S., Nance, B. and Moriarty, V. (2007) *Effective Teaching and Learning: Using ICT*. London: NRDC.

Moss, M. , Clark, A. and Thompson, S. (2007) *Adventures in Media Literacy*. Available for download from www.medialit.co.uk

Nance, B., Kambouri, M. and Mellar, H. (2007) *Using ICT, Developing adult teaching and learning: practitioner guides*. London: NRDC.

QCA (2007) *E-assessment: Guide to effective practice*. Available for download from www.efutures.org/docs/guide.pdf .

10
Appendix

Software for creating quizzes and assessment resources

Camstudio	www.camstudio.org
Create a Quiz	www.pc-shareware.com/quiz.htm
Custom Learning Studio	www.customcourse.com/index.asp
Dvolver	www.dfilm.com/live/mm.html
Exe Learning	http://exelearning.org/
Hot Potatoes	http://hotpot.uvic.ca/
Interactive Numeracy Materials	www.rkl.org.uk/llu/
MS Photo Story 3	www.microsoft.com/windowsxp/ using/digitalphotography/photostory /default.mspx
PictureGridEditor	www.tower.ac.uk/curweb/ resourcesdetail.asp?DocID=2148
PocketExam Software	www.bizon.org/pocketexam.tour
QuestionMark	www.questionmark.com/uk/ perception/index.aspx
QuestionTools	www.questiontools.com/
Quia	www.quia.com/
Quizzler Pro	www.quizzlerpro.com/
Quests2teach	www.aclresources.net/webquests/ index.html
Wink	www.debugmode.com/wink
Xerte	www.nottingham.ac.uk/xerte/